Unmasked

TRUDA ROSENBERG

Unmasked

Penumbra Press · Manotick, ON · 2009

In collaboration with the Zelikovitz Centre for Jewish Studies and
the Faculty of Arts and Social Sciences at Carleton University.

PENUMBRA PRESS, *publishers*
Box 940 | Manotick, ON | Canada
K4M 1A8 | penumbrapress.ca

Printed & bound in Canada

*Library and Archives Canada
Cataloguing-in-Publication Data*

Rosenberg, Gertruda (Truda)
   1922–
Unmasked / Gertruda Rosenberg.

"In collaboration with the Zelikovitz
Centre for Jewish Studies and the
Faculty of Arts and Social Sciences at
Carleton University."

ISBN 978-1-897323-37-3
   1. Rosenberg, Gertruda, 1922–.
   2. Holocaust, Jewish (1939–1945) –
   Personal narratives.
   3. Jews – Identity.
   4. Holocaust survivors – Canada –
   Biography.
   I. Max and Tessie Zelikovitz Centre for
   Jewish Studies
   II. Carleton University. Faculty of Arts
   and Social Sciences
   III. Title.

D804.196.R68 2009   940.53'18092
   C2009-902726-7

In blessed memory of all those
who were murdered during the Shoah,
lest they be annihilated.

Acknowledgements

I AM GRATEFUL TO ALL my friends who periodically
encouraged me to begin writing. One of them being
Dr. Hania Fedorowicz, who on occasion used her tape
recorder as an aid in making sure that I shall like to
hear myself talk Polish. It did not produce results but
encouraged thought.

Most of all, I am grateful to Annie Elliott, who simply
brought her computer and encouraged me to dictate to her
whatever I managed to scribble on paper. It became a routine
assignment. I had to produce the stories – simply because
I had to provide material for her to record, tidy pages, bind
them, read them over. Her encouragement and actual
execution of typing brought about a work discipline and
resulted in the collection of stories you are about to read.
I would still be postponing the task of writing had Annie
Elliott not persisted and encouraged my duty to 'produce.'

T.R.

Contents

FOREWORD

I am part of all that I have met;
Yet all experience is an arch wherethrough
Gleams that untraveled world, whose margin fades
For ever and for ever when I move.

OVER THE COURSE OF OUR LIVES, each one of us, like Ulysses in Tennyson's poem, meets many thousands of other human beings, fellow travellers in the adventure of life. Sometimes the meeting is fleeting, and sometimes our paths will intersect again on multiple occasions. If we are lucky, some of those whom we encounter will affect us profoundly, transforming what we believe and indeed changing who and what we are. When we, like Zbigniew Jasinski, look into that 'lopsided mirror' of our soul, these are the faces whose reflections we see.

I have been blessed in life by the opportunity to meet and engage with a great many remarkable people, whose company I have enjoyed and from whom I have learned enormously. Without a second's hesitation, I can say that Dr. Truda Rosenberg stands at the very top of that list. Others have inspired me by their ideals, their dedication or their perseverance, but Truda represents – more than anyone else

I know – the quiet triumph of the human spirit in the face of unimaginable adversity and unfathomable evil. She embodies all that is best about the human race. This is not some story from a film script or a novel but the actual experience of a woman who now sits so calmly and jokes with me across the table. From one point of view, our banter seems surreal; from another, utterly reassuring. How many people have I met who have jumped from a moving train carrying them to a death camp? How many people do I know who have been sold as a slave? As it happens, not that many. Indeed, only one. Hers is a story that must never be forgotten nor allowed to fade. While at first glance, it is a simple memoir of how a young Jewish girl from Lwów managed to survive the calamitous decade of the 1940s, it is so very much more than that. Like a Beethoven symphony, it transcends the specifics of times and place, a hymn to the power of goodness, a celebration of that spark of divine creation that we call so simply "life."

I write these words on the day that in Canada we celebrate Thanksgiving; indeed, there is much for which to be thankful. I shall hope that all readers of this book will pause for a moment and give thanks that some eighty-six years ago, the world witnessed the birth of Gertruda Osterman, who has been bearing witness to the human condition ever since.

John Osborne
Dean
Faculty of Arts and Social Sciences
Carleton University

1 | Over the River

It was not until March 1961 that I was confronted by my own very painful memories and experiences which happened between 1939 and 1942. It was my first touch with Israel, my holy land, the longing and dream of my people fulfilled.

There was a death in my husband's family and the nearest relatives were sitting shivah for seven days. Although a sad situation, it afforded us the opportunity to meet many old acquaintances and friends who according to Jewish custom were visiting the bereaved continually. One day, I noticed a woman who bore a striking resemblance to a man to whom I had been engaged many years ago and who like his father and brother were killed by the Nazis. I crossed the room to speak to her: "Excuse me." I said, "I can't help looking at you persistently but you remind me of the man I was about to marry in Poland during the early years of the Second World War. His name was Lolek Hubler." The woman turned pale and replied, "He was my brother's son."

The Soviet Army marched into the east of Poland in 1939. I was finishing high school and later entered my first year of university, which was ending in June 1941. Under the Soviet regime, my family, like many others, suffered financial hardship. It became incumbent upon me to take on a part-time job in an engineering firm. Lolek Hubler, a civil engineer, was an executive there. He soon noticed that mathematics, to be exact, even arithmetic, was not my strength. I was having serious problems with calculating as well as dealing with machinery, which led him to offer me his assistance. A beautiful, as well as meaningful relationship developed and led to an engagement. As a result, the members of the two families became acquainted. This was a pleasant development within difficult and uncertain times when people tended to cling to each other, hence to feel safer. The end of June 1941 marked the German invasion of our city, Lwów. We began to realize the unbelievable, that the very lives of all Jews were in serious danger. We began to consider ways of escaping Poland. Lolek's family had relatives in Argentina, which to us became our ultimate dream destination.

As the first step toward leaving Poland, Lolek and his brother Edek moved to Kosów, a small resort town in southeastern Poland that happened to have been my birthplace. Their father was settled at the same time in Kuty with one of my aunts and her son Joel. Using false identity papers, both Lolek and Edek found jobs. Lolek became an administrator of a hospital. He insisted that I join them. This was only the first phase of the intended move to Argentina via Romania, which was easily accessible from Kuty.

I hoped to escape detection as a Jew, was given Aryan identity papers and became Kazimiera Ostrowska, a Catholic girl. It was not an easy task to live anxiety-free when there were many Nazi collaborators who scrutinized everybody new to their vicinity. It took only a few weeks before I was suspected of being Jewish. The three of us were arrested, investigated and luckily released after a few days in the local prison. This incident became a strong incentive to plan the escape seriously. We hired a horse-driven carriage and travelled to Kuty in order to decide on the course of action with the help of my family and the senior Mr. Hubler.

I knew Kuty quite well. As a child I had attended elementary school there from grade one to four. I learned to swim in the Czeremosz River and spent many vacations with close friends who, as I did, moved away to other cities as they grew older and were in need of higher schooling.

It was my cousin Joel who knew the surrounding area very well and offered to show us a way of escape across the Czeremosz River into Romania. Joel guided us into the forest and stayed with us all night. Just as dawn was breaking, he led us to a shallow spot surrounding a small island. It seemed simple. We were able to walk in waist-high water and we saw the Romanian side as very close and accessible. The current was strong, and in the dim light of dawn we took a wrong turn and found ourselves, to our horror, back on the Polish side.

We repeated the exercise and managed to reach the Romanian soil. We were seized at once by Romanian soldiers and taken to a large hall, full of other Jews, all of whom had similar hopes as ours. There was a heavy silence. We just looked at one another with eyes reflecting hopelessness and despair. We suddenly realized that hospitality was not to be expected of our captors. We were noticing very quiet and successful attempts of murder/suicide with the help of morphine and cyanide. This I witnessed at close range and watched with sadness a physician whom I knew inject his wife and children with morphine followed by his swallowing a pill. The whole family was dead within a short time.

Nobody spoke, nobody cried. There was a frightening numbness interrupted at intervals by soldiers gathering some of us and leading us out of the hall. People were leaving their belongings and moving at the tempo dictated by our captors.

Suddenly, I was told by Lolek that he and his brother were going to put me into an armoire. It was a desperate attempt to save my life. They quickly shut the door and they were taken away.

My hiding place remained safe for a little while. It was a soldier's greed that betrayed me. He had a rifle slung over his shoulder, resting on his back with the bayonet pointing upward. He bobbed as he bent over to collect the unexpected loot, consisting of belongings left behind by those of us already taken away. His bayonet caught the door of the armoire, slightly opening it and there I was. He summoned another soldier to help him bind my wrists and then my ankles together, to run a pole through the shackles and carry me off, like a carcass of a slaughtered calf, to join the others waiting to cross the Czeremosz River in the direction of Kuty.

Edek and Lolek were in the crowd. We were all counted and again assembled in Kuty on the grounds of the very school I attended as a little girl.

It was a strange experience. We were afraid to move because we were strictly warned by soldiers not to dare move. We were even afraid to talk with one another while sitting or standing in one position and waiting for the next sequence of orders and manoeuvres by the watchful guards. It seemed that we became resigned, dull automatons, prisoners deprived of every human right to the extreme of having bodily movements curtailed.

2 | Kol Nidre

I AM WRITING THIS STORY on September 5TH, 2007, the sixty-fifth anniversary of the day I jumped out of the cattle train moving toward Belzec, the death camp in which half a million Jews were killed.

Most of my family was destroyed there. All victims' bodies were burned on the open field that constituted the camp. The people were literally shoved out from the cattle trains and beaten to a trot in order to reach their final destination, the actual gas chamber, as quickly as possible.

It may be appropriate at this point to introduce the process of bringing people to their final destination, one which I experienced – the cattle-train journey and the Death March.

Imagine a large crowd of people being pushed out from a school yard after a night spent on the ground, unprotected from the autumn weather, forbidden any change of position, not supplied with even the most primitive necessities for the most basic physiological needs, a crowd sitting or lying on the bare asphalt waiting for the next unknown and frightening circumstances.

For me personally, that schoolyard was a familiar space on which I spent many wonderful playful hours as a pupil.

We were all tired, unwashed, uncombed, hungry, thirsty and above all frightened and sad. Imagine men, women, children of all ages including babies in their mothers' arms; all of us were pushed together and out onto a rough road, forced by many guards to keep to an orderly set of columns and reasonably rhythmic march. The accompanying yelling of the guards demanding order and established by them, a desired speed, must be left to the ability of the reader to envision and comprehend.

As I write, I am assuring myself of the ability in providing a believable picture because, after all, I was there – one of the mass of human beings subjected by other humans to behaviours ranging from attempts to remain sensible, seeming to become automatons without a murmur of revolt. Indeed I was there … with others as young as I who were trying hard to keep up; no, not just keep up but help others to carry on. It needs to be explained that if one stumbled, slowed down or fell, a bullet or hard kick by the guard would result in being drawn out of the walking crowd, left dead or dying on the side of the road. An attempt to help, when noticed by the guards would be punished. I recall that those of us who were not only young enough but also strong and compassionate, as much as able to disregard the consequences of the oppressing brutality, established unwittingly, intuitively a uniform, unnoticeable manoeuvre in helping others to march on: by actual physical support, such as taking a baby out of a mother's arms or holding up an elderly person to prevent a fall.

As we moved on, we found many bodies left on the road. The tragic moments, remembered forever, were those in which any outward reaction to these sights had to be muted.

It has to be remembered that on many occasions one's loved ones have fallen victim to the senseless brutality – and unless we were prepared to share their fate, people within the Death March had to move on.

In that tragic shuffle, I spotted my two aunts, both sisters of my mother. Only our eyes met as we dared to hope that we would be together ... as it happened, we were directed to the same spot and were able to huddle together for the journey inside the cattle train.

There may have been enough space within the wagon for about forty cattle. I have an idea of some one hundred to one hundred and fifty people who were there within this particular wagon. There were no toilets, there was no water and there was certainly no food. There was only meagre air reaching some of us depending on our positions in relation to the small openings at the height suitable for cows and horses. The train was moving slowly often turning onto side railway tracks, backing up, moving forward, stopping ... all in attempt to frustrate, tire and dehumanize us, forcing behaviours marked by regression as well as despair. The cries, the yells, the desperate attempts to remain quiet, all mingled with hope that somehow, somebody would help. We were often hopeful when nearing a railway station that passengers, awaiting their scheduled trains, would help. We were begging for water; we were throwing out whatever we still had as payment: a wedding band, a watch, a blouse, a dress, a coat. Some would undress and remain naked in order to contribute to their payment for rescue or even a drink of water! The people on the platforms looked, observed as one does when circus animals are being transported. There was no visible compassion, no anger, no relating to those of us being transported.

Attempts to drink one's own urine were becoming more frequent and obvious. The heat, the stench and continual bold, painful noise were the constant ecology. We sat on the floor most of the time since there was no room for movement. At one point, I tried to lean against the wagon wall and remained in that position for hours. Two men noticed me with the resulting cautious approach and question: "If we help you to jump from here, would you consider it?" I slid down to the floor, looked at my aunts questioningly, they heard the proposal to help me jump. Both of them looked at me; the elder one reached to her hair, recovered a bracelet and proceeded to nestle it into my thick hair. Then, speaking slowly and quietly said, "Jump, child." The younger one did not respond verbally. She gave me a quick hug. The two men helped me up, lifted me to the opening, turned me into the prone position and pushed me through. My head was still inside the wagon and the rest of me was clinging to the outside of it. I was clutching the ledge of the wagon opening. The cattle train was moving forward slowly, my eyes focusing on my two beloved aunts. The two men watched for the right moment to shout; "Jump!"

Suddenly, my younger aunt began to chant. The terrible chaos stopped. The only audible voice was the voice of my beloved Aunt Rosa. The chant was *Kol Nidre – All Vows*. She chanted in Hebrew the following prayer:

> *Let all our vows, all oaths, all the promises we make and*
> *the obligation we incur to you, O God, between this day*
> *of atonement until the next, be null and void should we*
> *after honest effort find ourselves unable to fulfil them,*
> *then may we be absolved of them.*

The prayer stopped and I heard the order, "Jump!" And jump I did, backwards! I rolled down the embankment, lifted my head just enough to see the train moving away and some uniformed men standing on the platform with guns ready to shoot ... but they didn't.

For years, I have wondered why my aunt chanted this particular prayer. She knew its meaning in the context of Jewish history, persecutions, bondage, lack of freedom to be Jews and no freedom to make one's own decisions, being forced to say what they would not mean, to say yes when no would have been more appropriate.

She must have feared that I would not be able to live as a Jew, were I to survive. Were I to die, she would have prayed for forgiveness of my shortcomings.

IT WAS NOT UNTIL THE YEAR 2005 that I was able to visit the Belzec Death Camp, which today stands as a memorial to people who were killed there. Their bodies were burned on the open field after being gassed. There are no lists of names belonging to the victims because we were shoved into the trains, counted, and the number was written in white paint on the outside of the wagon; a fact which adds to the sorrowful reality of a brutal attitude towards Jews – subhumans, in the eyes of the Nazis! There at Belzec Death Camp, a sign bearing a message with the inscription in three languages contains a plea:

> *Earth, do not cover my blood:*
> *Let there be no resting place for my outcry!*

3 | After the Jump

THERE I WAS, AT THE FOOT of the embankment, conscious of the physical displacement and dire thirst. Nothing was hurting. There was no discomfort. It was difficult to acknowledge the cattle train had gone by and I was alive fully dressed in a brick-coloured suit, shoes and a black silk kerchief around my neck.

Since the field in front of me was rather difficult to negotiate in high heels, I removed them, transforming my kerchief into a carrying satchel. As I took the first steps into the field, the scene felt unreal; I remember being in a daze, not quite aware of how or where to turn. It was a warm, late September afternoon, the railway tracks were behind me, the field in front of me was promising peace and security, yet the scene on my right soon became bizarre: a few, perhaps two or three, naked people distant from one another, covering themselves with leafy tree branches, stood, moved cautiously, then disappeared, then reappeared – nobody spoke. We noticed one another without uttering a sound, afraid to interact. Slowly, I found myself entering the field. As if out of nowhere, a young peasant woman carrying a pail was walking towards me, which made me hope that she may be carrying water. She was indeed! It was not quite clear to me whether it was safe to stop her, yet the risk had to be taken: "May I please have a drink of water?" I pleaded. There was no response. The woman kept walking slowly. She seemed to have compassion. At least that is what I felt or wanted to hear. In desperation, I dared to gesture that I wanted her to set the pail on the ground but she just stood there and let me do it. I knelt down, tipped the pail and took a long drink of the precious water. As she stood there watching me, I realized that she must have been a deaf mute. At this point we began to understand each other. Motioning me to follow her, she led me into a little field-hut and offered a baked field potato, which I ate greedily under her watchful eye. As soon as I took the final bite, she indicated that I should follow her, and I did.

By this time it was dusk; the young woman led me a considerable distance and indicated a spot where she suggested I ought to lie down. It was a bushy undergrowth with a few reeds nearby. She saw me sit down, must have been satisfied, with acceptance smiled rather shyly and left abruptly. I was well hidden and able to lie down, almost ready to sleep.

As darkness fell, I began to hear shouting, German-sounding orders calling out, dogs howling. It was not difficult to assess that the Germans were out with their bloodhounds looking for their victims. Of course, I was one of their targets as was anyone who may have escaped from the cattle train. There was no time to ruminate, think, plan. I was tired and was thankfully falling asleep. To this day, I remember the dream in which someone was covering me with a warm blanket. Of course, in reality, no one did. Upon wakening, I was happy to find the sun shining and realized that I must move on. To my amazement, I had spent the night at the edge of a swamp that prevented my discovery by the dogs and the uniformed murderers. The peasant woman knew exactly what she was doing when she brought me there the night before. She was not to be found again in the morning.

It took a little time to make the decision to exchange my attire for peasant-like clothing, if at all possible. There were a few homes in the nearby neighbourhood, a lucky situation, which made it possible to enquire where such an exchange could take place. I did knock at the nearest door, which was hospitably opened while a most important question was asked, namely: "Why was I there?" and "Why did I jump from the train?" – to which another untrue story had to be invented: "I was on the train with my Jewish husband, but did not want to die. I am trying to make my way home and prefer to be in peasant clothing." I then proceeded to ask whether they would consider making an exchange. The peasants liked the idea; supplied a long heavy linen embroidered shirt and a dark green dress to go over it. My costume was perfect.

As I was changing dresses, I noticed that the very much cherished silver locket, which I hid in my bra encasing photographs of my parents, was lost. This hurt. More so did the terrible reality of my two beloved aunts continuing their journey to death. I was hoping that my mother would be still alive in the Lwów Ghetto. I was leaving the peasants who were kind enough to replace my shoes with ten hard-boiled eggs for my barefoot march toward Lwów.

The road was bearable but the journey painful. I came across groups of Jewish slaves labouring on the road, crushing large stones into gravel with bare hands. They were drawn, pale, tired and sad. As I walked by them, I rolled the hard-boiled eggs towards them and walked on inconspicuously watching their surprise, as much as careful attempts to share the few bites without curiosity about their source. That was very sad. Yet an even greater sadness was caused by the appearance of a little boy in my path. He must have been five or six years old, dark haired and brown eyed; his pleading I shall never forget: "Lady, please lady, take me with you … I have some money." I stopped, showed him the peasant houses and directed him towards them. I walked away and did not look back.

Where could I have taken him? I assumed that his parents threw him out of the train to save his life. Many parents did this, at that time. To this day, I look into the eyes of every man known to have survived the Shoah and hope that the little boy grew into one of them. Perhaps I could have taken care of him … the memory is painful and will be as long as I live.

THE ABOVE STORY IS ONE of many terrible things the Nazis caused to happen to my people. Parents were abandoning their children in the struggle for survival, both their own and that of their offspring. The Nazi standpoint was to destroy us as sub-human creatures and they were making subhumans of us before the final murder, a reality difficult to comprehend. Where was the rest of the world? The expression of the dark-eyed little boy still haunts me to this day; his pleading voice, "Lady, please lady, take me with you," rings clear in my memory.

The fact remains: I kept walking away and did not look back.

4 | THE GHETTO

IT WAS FALL. LEAVES WERE becoming colourful and the days were shorter. We were informed by posters throughout the city of Lwów that Jews were not allowed to live next to their non-Jewish neighbours – a ghetto was being established only for us Jews.

The feverish planning under our new conditions began. We gave away most, if not all, of our furniture including the piano without which I felt deprived of a life support: yet nothing was tragic in my perception of the strange unknown.

We were to move into a room that in time became occupied by other members of our family. There was hardly enough room to move.

My mother and I were alone. My father was not with us anymore. He was taken away a few months earlier with many of his colleagues and other professionals. At a much later date we learned they were shot on the grounds of the local prison.

We were carrying things out and placing them into a hand-drawn cart which could only hold the 'bare necessities.' It was difficult to estimate what exactly the term represented. Be as it may, we packed it full. To save the contents from spilling over the top, we decided that I should sit on the top of the 'piled-in stuff' to keep it together with my outstretched arms and body.

I positioned myself for this important task when my mother was approaching to take hold of the long handle with which she was going to drag the cart. She suddenly stopped and uttered almost in a panic: "Oh, I forgot something very important." She ran back and appeared a few moments later carrying a large bottle of Evening in Paris cologne. We looked at one another. What my mother saw was me holding on to whatever we could pack into the cart sitting on top of the pile, arms outstretched and wearing a green fez-like hat with a long feather in it. What I saw was my mother with the most unlikely 'important piece of our possessions' in her hands. We burst out laughing – a laughter that turned into tearful crying, utterance of grief, fear and helplessness in the face of cruel reality. She drew the four-wheeled cart for quite a distance through the elegant streets of Lwów from where we lived, until we reached the rundown area in the poor section of the city, a mixture of small factories, a small synagogue, cellars, little schools, little shops, coffee houses and workmen's households to be occupied on a 'first come, first served' basis, utilized by us Jews as living quarters.

The address was 35 Zamarstynowska Street, which was an old soda-water factory, no longer a factory but made into rooms and small suites. The bare necessities were available, depending on demand, which often seemed disproportionate to the space. The grounds around the building were quite large and quickly occupied by furniture pieces, folding beds, carts, baby carriages and toys. Nothing seemed to resemble regular space usage, nothing made sense. We were fortunate to have been offered a room, just a room which may have been adequate for two people; the space was quickly filled with four more! We were told that the cellar would be for the convenience of all of us in case of need to hide, rest, or sleep when there was no room anywhere else. At that time, November 1941, the ghetto was still open – anybody could come in and we were able to exit as long as we were displaying the ten-centimetres-wide armband on our right sleeve.

It was a very strange and dangerous place. Anybody could rob, beat, kill or take us away and we had no recourse. The freedom we had was conditional on the kindness, or lack of it, of the visiting multiethnic representatives. There were Germans, Ukrainians and Christian Poles. Some would come to sell us vegetables, fruit and other food for cash or any valuables they preferred. Clothing was also a profitable bartering item. Ghetto life is portrayed better by writers who have researched all pertinent details of its administration and interaction with the governing German authorities whose main aim was the destruction of the ghetto population. We had to be sensitive and vigilant in order to minimize the speed by which they were advancing their cause.

There were many, constant dangers of being caught and directed to do all kinds of tasks without having the security of returning. It was frighteningly real. I was caught, taken out of the ghetto and bodily taken to a prison where I and others had to clean corridors and toilets with bare hands, forced to look and listen to the incarcerated, who were rough as much as rude criminals, making themselves heard behind bars. The day finally came to an end. I returned to the ghetto to find my mother frantic with fear about my absence, unable to offer anything to stave off my hunger and exhaustion. She reluctantly offered me two cigarettes which she scrounged somewhere. I learned that day that cigarettes subdue hunger.

On another occasion, with a similar absence, my poor mother ran toward me with an anxious, urgent report about our close neighbours, a rabbi and his wife, having been taken away to an 'Umschlagplatz' which was known to pre-empt further displacement. She pleaded with me, "Trudenko, do something!" And something I did. I dared to change very quickly to look presentable. I approached the camp guards in fluent German, with a two-handled basket in hand and requested two people to help me deliver bread rations for the camp. Of course it was a blatant lie, a scheme. My German was flawless. I looked German and was credible. One guard offered to find two people for me but I informed him that I preferred to choose the two people myself. Of course, I chose the rabbi and his wife. We left quickly. When we reached the ghetto, I was thanked by them in a beautiful, unforgettable manner. The rabbi placed his hand on my head and recited a blessing which in translation is:

> May God *bless you and guard you;*
> May God *show you favour and be gracious to you;*
> May God *show you kindness and grant you peace.*

I left the ghetto later in the fall, in November, upon my mother's insistence. She wanted me to live!

Diseases were rampant. Fleas, bed bugs and lice were plentiful and indestructible. I always had a clean head of hair in the morning but by every evening lice would be found in my hair and two in my bra. My hair was never more beautiful though before or after the Shoah because of the constant use of oil of sassafras. Typhus was widespread!

I decided to volunteer at the Jewish hospital within the ghetto. It was in essence a hospital for Jews – a difference implied by the names. There were no nurses, few physicians, no laboratories; neither was there medication nor food. Periodically, the Germans, helped by the Askaris, would enter the ghetto, including the hospital, with the sole purpose of killing as many people as possible.

In the spring of 1942, I was nineteen years old. At the hospital, I was what one would call, under normal circumstances, in a normal Western-world hospital, a candy striper, and was performing duties as needed, such as assisting patients but also doing menial work such as cleaning and scrubbing floors. These circumstances also provided the opportunity for me and the others to enjoy the occasional skimpy meal or a hot shower when available. On many occasions we would bring food and share it with the patients. There really wasn't much to share. We were mostly hungry – patients and staff alike. Yet there was somehow the feeling of being safe within the hospital walls. The logical assumption was that the sick would be allowed to heal if only for the continual supply of slave labour.

One day, we the caregivers were warned that one of the infamous 'Aktionen,' meaning 'actions,' by the Germans was to take place. The German actions were quite frequent within the ghetto and resulted always in the reduction of the ghetto population. The threat was real. Results were known. A desperate need to save family members, children in particular, drove some of us to attempt the prevention of the expected murders. Some staff members brought with them their children, babies amongst them, in an effort to save them from death. I remember vividly the tense speed at which we applied splints and bandages to the tiny legs, arms, chests and heads respectively to make them look like surgical patients in the hope that nobody would dare to touch, abuse or beat the little people in a hospital setting.

We worked feverishly until an order was issued to take up our positions in our respective wards so that no ward would be left unattended.

The SS and Askaris had just entered the hospital. I ran to my ward. Picture the ward. Two rows of beds with some twenty-five men in them swollen from hunger, bruised from beatings, pinned to their beds by surgical contraptions and Smith-Petersen nails through their limbs to hold them in a steady state. Picture a piercing silence and helplessly frightened eyes. Listen to shrieks of children and babies in the background. Hear the blood-curdling yells of the Germans and see the door fling open as three uniformed executioners enter the ward with a thundering "H'Raus, H'Raus, H'Raus!" When there was no response and no movement by those pinned to their beds, the three began to throw the mattresses with the patients on them to the floor. It does not take a great deal of imagination to feel and hear their pain!

There I was, one of them – incapable of a positive action, frightened myself, but standing as if in charge ... perhaps I was! I heard these patients' pain, mingled with the brutal yells of the German executioners and decided that we were all about to die. I intoned the 'Shema':

> Shema Yisrael,
> Adonai Eloheinu,
> Adonai echad.

(Hear, O Israel. The Lord is our God. The Lord is one!)

The patients, some of them under their mattresses on the floor, continued the prayer: (in the Ashkenazi pronunciation)

> Boruch shem kwod
> Malchuso
> Leoylem wued.

(Blessed is His glorious Kingdom forever and ever!)

I did not know the words. They did. The executioners stopped. They stood there motionless for a short moment and then, one of them slapped my face once, then twice more, and left the ward. The door slammed shut and the prayer continued. I heard the voices of my patients:

We ahavto as Adojnoj
Eloheho b'hol levaveho
U'b'hol nafsheho u'b'hol meodeho.

(You shall love the Lord your God with all your mind,
with all your strength, with all your being.)

These patients survived the day. There were numerous bodies all over the hospital: children with smashed heads, the elderly, everybody was lying around. I do not recall if some of the staff were missing. I did not know all of them.

The actions of the SS were brutal, quick and merciless.

TO THIS DAY, I AM TRYING to understand how any civilized population can turn into brutal automatons in the deed of killing. What is even more unbelievable is that many of the commanders had doctorates. Doctorates of what? Instruction in what subject? It became obvious to me that none of them could have been educated within the true meaning of the word.

5 | THE LAST EMBRACE

I T WAS NOVEMBER 2, 1942, at 5:00 AM, a cold dark morning at the wall of the Lwów Ghetto. My mother stood facing me, her arms on my shoulders, her eyes looking at me intently as if ready to assess my strength, endurance and possibly courage. She started haltingly, "Trudenko, many things will be happening to your body. I know that you will deal with it."

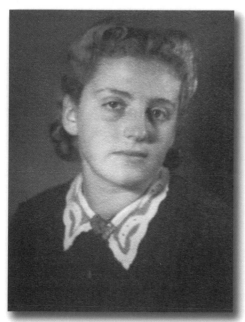

— *1942*

She drew me closer. My head was now on her left shoulder. No, I did not cry. I turned my head and straightened my shoulders. I looked into her eyes wanting to absorb the blueness, the penetrating softness and expression of trust and care. "Trudenko," she repeated, "don't let anything happen to your Jewish soul."

One more hug and I left the gate of the ghetto. The train for Warsaw was to leave soon.

6 | WARSAW

EQUIPPED WITH A VERY SMALL SUITCASE and satchel, dressed in a very simple light woollen dress, tweed coat and a felt hat large enough to cover my curly hair, I joined my mother's cousin with her little son, Stefanek, and boarded the train as Zofia Wolanowska on my way to Warsaw.

ZBIGNIEW JASINSKI

— 1942

Warsaw seemed to many of us big enough, impersonal enough and therefore safe enough to disappear into, with a false identity within the Aryan population.

It seemed to us that the risk of being recognized as Jewish was much less in a big city, where no one would have known us personally. The journey was uneventful except for anxiety and hunger that one had to deal with in order to appear comfortable and relaxed. We did not speak to one another. We were careful not to draw undue attention to ourselves; I was mostly pretending to be drowsy.

At one point, I thought or dreamt that I had a sandwich in my satchel. I reached down, began going through my belongings but to no avail, there was no sandwich there. Indeed, there was not! To my horror, what I found was my Jewish Kennkarte, the notorious ID card designed for Jews only, with my real name on it. It caused a shock which could have resulted in confusion had I not remembered a meaningful incident of my mother's concern for the importance of one's true identity. It stems from the time of July 15, 1941, when a Nazi order was issued for Jews to wear a ten-centimetres-wide white armband with a blue Star of David on it.

My mother prepared my armband. She embroidered the Star of David and proceeded to place it on my right sleeve. "Wear it with pride," she said. The armband identification was just the beginning of the outward marking of Jews. At that time, nobody even suspected all that would transpire and the calculated cruelties that eventually ensued with the intention to annihilate the Jews.

On one occasion I decided to leave the band off and dared to step out of the ghetto. My mother followed me at a safe distance without my knowledge until I just happened to look back and notice her. I questioned my mother's actions and she replied, "If anything should happen to you, Trudenko, it must be clear that you are a Jew! It must be clear who you are!"

Now, back on the train to Warsaw, what was I to do with my Jewish ID? Throwing it out, even in pieces, could have been dangerous. With all these thoughts racing through my mind, I proceeded, very inconspicuously, to tear the cardboard-like ID into tiny pieces and when small enough, I chewed them up, bit by bit until they were soft enough to be swallowed and that I did. Every last shred of evidence was gone!

The train arrived in Warsaw. Another cousin was waiting for us. I saw her from a distance but avoided waving to her while she was greeting her sister with little Stefanek.

At that very moment, without any warning, I was approached by two uniformed Polish militiamen who stopped me rather abruptly. These people were known to be working in collaboration with the Nazis. One of them grabbed my suitcase, sharply accused me of being Jewish and announced they were taking me for interrogation. While walking to our destination, nobody talked. At the entrance to a large, ugly red-brick fortress-like building, I asked, "Where are we?" They answered in unison, "Pawiak!"

This being my first time in Warsaw, I did not know the significance of Pawiak. I understood it to be a landmark in the city. What's more, I was very curious as to who would be interrogating me. We then entered a small bright room with a desk and a chair or two. One of the men sat down at the desk while the other was opening my suitcase and examining its contents.

"You are a Jew," charged one of the militiamen, rather brashly. To this day, I can hardly believe the wit and audacity demonstrated in my response. "Now listen carefully," I retorted as I looked at my watch to somehow give the impression that

I was in a hurry. "I may have many sins but being Jewish is not one of them!" I was telling the absolute truth!

"Why did you come to Warsaw?" the other asked sharply. "Actually, I am looking for a job," I replied. The next statement by the man at the desk was thrown at me harshly. "If you are not a Jew, then you must observe Advent."

"Do you?" I asked, "Only the very religious do. I don't come from a very religious family."

One of them asked, "So, what is Advent?" The question was repeated.

"Don't you know," I wondered, "why are you asking me? Aren't you Catholic?"

At that moment, I noticed a German sign on the door leading to another office. I inquired, "Where does this lead to?"

"They are the German police. You will be going there next" was their response.

At that moment, I became very frightened but attempted to keep my cool, looked at my watch and said, "I have an appointment in an hour. You are keeping me here. God knows why. I may lose my chance of a job. Would you please take me to the tram station as quickly as you can? If you send me next door, what would be your reward? If you take me to the tram car, you will have a surprise as a thank-you."

I dared to say something more: "I wouldn't want to be in your shoes when we meet after the war. So let's hurry." The militia man asked what number of tram I needed. "Any number will do, hurry," was my reply. He helped me with my valise. I stepped onto the first tramcar without a clue where it would take me. As the tramcar was rolling away, I carefully pulled out of my hair a gold bracelet with three one-karat diamonds that my aunt gave me on the cattle train. I pitched it carefully for him to catch, and he did, just in time and let me see his salute.

It was not until much later that I realized what Pawiak was all about. The Pawiak is best described by those who lived through it, survived its horrors and were fortunate enough not to have been tortured to death.

I was able to orient myself as to the direction I needed to take in order to arrive at an address where people were prepared to extend a helping hand to my kind of 'criminal.' I found the way to Mrs. Faliszewska, the wife of a well-known Polish actor by the same name. I knocked at her door, she quickly opened it and greeted me with a warm "Come in child." She told me that I could spend a few days in safety but she would not be able to feed me. In the same breath, this wonderful lady suggested that my hair was too different from the usual blond of Polish-Aryan girls and I needed to have it treated immediately. There was urgency in her voice that she confirmed by giving me the address of the hairdresser she wanted me to see at once. Time and timing were of essence. I followed her suggestion without delay.

The room was tiny, very clean and tidy. The professional atmosphere was reflected in attention to detail given to a well-maintained hairdresser chair, tools, washbasin and a curtain which was meant to create 'The Hairdressing Corner.' The remainder of the room was simply furnished as a bed-sitting room and kitchen corner, distinguished by a two-burner cooking plate, a very small cupboard and a square table.

I stood at the door informing the very neat elderly lady that I was sent by Madame Faliszewska. She smiled, showed me to the hairdressing chair and assured me that she knew what to do. In a most difficult moment, I informed her that I had no money, to which she smiled again and took my hand as if to say, "Do not worry." The procedure of dyeing my hair was soon under way. The little lady was working gently and lovingly.

ZBIGNIEW JASINSKI

— 1942

Tired, exhausted, sad and hungry, I fell asleep in the middle of the process to be woken up by the wonderful smell of a barley soup which she held close to my face. Her voice softly said, "Eat my child. You must be very hungry." As she watched me eating slowly with care not to spill any of the cherished broth, she inquired, "Where are you going to stay?" "I shall look for work whilst I am with Madame Faliszewska but I have no idea where I am going to stay." She eagerly replied: "I have a sister here in the next tower. Come with me. She may be able to help."

We did see her sister and without any hesitation she invited me to share her apartment. Money? I had none. "Stay as long as you want," she remarked, "but I can give you nothing to eat." I was grateful and expressed it. The lady showed me a chaise-longue in her living room which I could use as a bed. She indicated that there was no bedding available. It amazes me now that nothing like that worried me.

On that very first evening, we were sitting at the dining-room table drinking a mixture of chicory and boiled water which we called coffee. It was a moment of rest and reprieve from a very long and intense day. Suddenly, the entrance door opened and a gentleman entered. At that instant, my heart began to race as it had on so many other occasions. Living under an assumed identity provoked a state of anxiety in almost every situation. "What now," I thought. The man stopped to greet us. The landlady introduced me and said: "This is Zofia Wolanowska, Mr. Jasinski. She came from Lwów, escaping from the German Arbeitsamt (German Department of Labour). She is looking for work. Can you help?"

Zbigniew Jasinski looked at me with a warm smile, turned toward a door, unlocked it and disappeared inside his room. Some half an hour later he joined us for a moment, displayed a brown paper bag and uttered the following: "I would like to take you to lunch tomorrow at 1:00 PM. We will talk about finding you a job." As he was talking, he opened the brown bag and spread the open space on the table with a large amount of chocolate and sweets, announcing, "This is on account." He bid us goodnight and left the apartment.

Zbigniew Jasinski appeared at 1:00 PM the next day as he had promised. We walked into a small restaurant. He chose the table and pulled up a chair, gestured for me to sit in such a way that my back was to the people in the restaurant whilst he sat opposite me with full view of the people and all that was happening around us. There was a window behind his back looking out onto a brick wall. Years later, when I recall that luncheon with Zbigniew Jasinski, I believe that he knew I was Jewish and was concerned for my safety. In those days, one could never be too careful as there were always people in the crowd who were searching, scrutinizing the surroundings with

ZBIGNIEW JASINSKI

— 1942

the intent to discover, expose and capture Jews. To this day, I am grateful at the thought of people like Jasinski and their kind gestures at the risk of their own lives.

Jasinski began by telling me that our landlady was a very decent but also naive human being. Her main occupation was fortune-telling, which brought all kinds of people into her home. He suggested that I would be much more comfortable and certainly more private in his room, which he occupied and used occasionally for the safe-keeping of his unpublished poems: he proposed that I keep his poetry well ordered and securely stored. Since he had no money at his disposal to pay for my services, he promised to send a young man, from a factory that he administered, with daily food supplies for the landlady and me. He handed over the key to his room and we returned together to acquaint me with its layout.

The room was tiny, very plain and modest. There was an iron bed in the corner. A little armoire stood next to the only window in the room. A very small white table with two drawers in it was propped against a bare wall with a mirror hung lopsidedly over it. There was a tiled coal-burning stove in the room; it was meant to heat two rooms; the one that we were in and also the adjoining living room with the chaise-longue in it. This stove held the promise of an inviting and friendly fire but it never warmed, at least not during my stay there.

Zbigniew Jasinski would come by from time to time and take me to visit his family. On one occasion, he wanted me to meet his wife, Wanda Karczewska. I met her only once. She was not very impressed with me to say the least. It was obvious that she did not wish to have me around.

I was very grateful for the privacy and safety of that little room. My stay there was somewhat brief. In the course of time, I found employment and began work as a maid, a mother's helper, a nanny, which made it possible for me to live in normal households.

On some occasions, I found myself involved in transporting weapons and munitions in preparation of the Warsaw Ghetto Uprising and later the Warsaw Uprising. Zbigniew Jasinski, the gentleman, poet and factory administrator, was a member of the Armia Krajowa (Home Army). To my surprise, I found this out many years later, in 1998, when I visited Yad Vashem, the Holocaust Memorial Museum in Israel – with the intention of having Jasinski's name included in the list of the names of the 'Righteous Gentiles.' To my astonishment, I discovered that he was the leader of the Rickshaw Brigade. His pseudo name was Rudy. The Brigade was using rickshaws as a means of transportation for carrying out covert operations and secret communications, all in preparation for the uprisings.

One day, I found myself on a tramcar carrying a violin case containing weapons. As I was standing and dragging the case along because it was just too heavy to carry, I became aware of a man looking at me very intently. My first thought was that he had recognized me as a Jew. Had I been caught, I had two death sentences against me: first for being a Jew, second for smuggling and carrying weapons. Thinking this could be my last hour or last chance of survival, having nothing to lose, I turned to him, pretended to be indignant at his lack of tact and manners and I sharply said, "You are staring at me!" To this he smiled and said, "You resemble so much the Holy Mary, Mother of God." It never occurred to me that he might have been looking at me because I was attractive! All I thought, at that moment, was that he should not know that Mary was Jewish!

— *1943*

Jasinski would weave his way in and out of my life. He would disappear sporadically and would suddenly reappear, which he did, the last time, a few days before the Warsaw Uprising began. He looked at me like an old friend would and said, "In a few days nobody will worry about who was who and why!" He handed me his latest photograph of 1944 and wrote on it: "May we meet again when man will no longer be wolf to man – affectionately Zbyszek." I have not seen him since.

In 1943, I watched the Warsaw Ghetto Uprising from my employer's window and was careful to hide not only my deep sadness but also enormous pride at the courage of my people, my brothers and sisters, young, old, children, the able and the disabled, being murdered for no other reason but that of being Jewish. I also witnessed the courage and compassion of the Christian Poles and was not able to express my thanks to them. I was sad and helpless but tried to make their tragedies bearable, when there was no way of expressing my own.

In 1944, the Warsaw Uprising ended in the destruction of the city and its population.

I was in the trenches looking for food; I cooked on my knees in order to avoid detection by snipers shooting from roofs across the street, all with the hope that the lives of parents on whom children depended would be preserved. It seemed to me that should I have died, no one would have missed me; my absence would not necessarily be noticed. Notwithstanding my thoughts, I gained strength and satisfaction by making it feasible for others to live.

Years later, in 1996, I happened to meet a Polish general and a Polish professor at the Polish Embassy in Ottawa. I asked them if they knew the poet Jasinski and if so, did they know what ever happened to him. Both of them knew him. They told me that he died in 1984, in Australia, and that there was a

— Zbigniew Jasinski, 1944

book about him; an Ottawa family knew him well and was in possession of the book. I contacted the family and ordered the book. To my astonishment, I found the following poem, called "Piosenka," which means "Little Song." It must have been written during the Uprising because as I found out later, he had been taken to Germany as a prisoner of war. The poem talks about the room I occupied for a while; in translation from Polish, it reads as follows:

> *It is empty in the tiny room*
> *Four bare walls*
> *A lopsided mirror*
> *And a stove which never warms ...*
> *Through the dirty panes, sadness looks into the window,*

And dust covers the cobwebs in its corners ...
And over the cobwebs
– so easily without effort at all –
Flow memories of you, my girl.
Somewhere in the burned city
Different walls of mine,
Resounded with the laughter out of different times ...
It is an empty sadness, futile thoughts and tears ...
I will have a drink, to somehow forget
Not to see; not to hear; not to think.
I will drink some more
And return drunk to my sadness
Within my empty walls ...
I will look in the mirror hung lopsided still –
The world will whirl around and in it
With my searching muddled eyes, I will see you.

7 | A Debt Paid

I T MUST HAVE BEEN LATE AUTUMN 1944. I was still strong in spirit, healthy despite all that had happened thus far. The prevailing conditions in Poland at that time were quite chaotic and I was mistaken for an East German refugee, although the Germans registered me as their slave under the auspices of the infamous Organization Todt. It was a frightening experience to have found myself in the company of Poles who were really German nationals. I was petrified to be recognized as a Jew. Even in the chaos which existed just before the German defeat, the biggest crime was still being a Jew.

I was among Germans when the plane landed in Frankfurt; we all lined up together and began climbing into a truck that was to take us out of the airport. At that very point, I truly panicked and had to deal with racing thoughts of possible interrogation. What then? An East German? What kind of East German? Where do you come from? In what city did you live? Where are your identification papers? Whom do you know? What is your destination? Why are you travelling with the refugees from Poland? Does anybody know you?

I managed to sneak away from the lineup without being questioned. Once again, I was on the run without knowing which way to turn; a bus arrived at the bus stop, Centre Town was its destination. I hopped onto the packed bus and noticed only one unoccupied seat which I aimed for. There sat a young woman. I began with a question in German: "Will you please excuse me? Would you know where I could find some accommodation for the night?" She answered quickly and cheerfully: "There are lots of places prepared for the East German refugees from Poland." I listened, thought for a while and decided to risk it: "You see, miss," I said in a whisper, slowly and carefully ... "I am not a German." The young woman looked at me questioningly and put one finger in front of her lips, motioned to me to stop speaking and said in a whisper, "Let's get out of here and talk as we walk on the street." At that very moment the ticket agent approached us. I had no money and she anticipated this, paid for me and gently took my hand saying, "Please come with me," which I did. She continued to talk whilst we were walking, "I live not far from here. My roommate will be quite happy to have you join us. You said that you are not a German. What nationality are you?" "I am Polish," I said and a few steps later added, "I can't possibly come with you." "Why is that?" she asked. "Because, though I am Polish, I am not a Christian Pole," I said. She stopped, waiting for me to continue, when I quietly explained: "I am a Jew. This is why I can't possibly accept your offer ... Your lives will be in danger because of me." At that point she firmly took my hand saying: "All the more reason why you should come with me." I hesitated and she continued: "You must come. I want you to have a rest."

I could not quite recall when I last enjoyed a bath with nice soap and steaming hot water, all in a nice bathroom and bathtub. I enjoyed the thought of clean linen and a soft pillow under my head.

Just when I was ready to retire, my hostess informed me that she needed to leave me for a few minutes in order to make a phone call. There was no telephone in her apartment. I had nothing to say but became worried that she might be calling the Gestapo in order to report the presence of a Jew in her apartment. The worry lasted for a very brief moment … it was not the first time that I had to deal with it. It became 'a constant' in view of my precarious status of a condemned person – condemned to death! I decided therefore that one can die only once and now is the time for me to die. At least, I thought, I had experienced some kindness, a warm home, a nice meal, all to be grateful for. Now, I concluded, she had to do her duty to her Fuehrer and help kill one more 'sub-human.' I did not react and remembered that I had successfully played the role of being at peace. My hostess gave no indication of whom she was going to call. She left and returned some minutes later with a big smile, saying: "I just called my mother in Berlin and she suggested that I take you out of here early in the morning, before the concierge of the building gets up and possibly notices a stranger. It could become a dangerous situation. We shall leave here before 4:00 AM and I will put you on the five-o'clock train for Berlin. My mother will be waiting for you on the platform. She will have a newspaper under her arm. Wait for my mother to approach you."

The young woman purchased my ticket and the train pulled away from the station in Frankfurt with me in it.

A lady with a newspaper under her arm waited for me in Berlin. She stretched out her hand to me and simultaneously introduced herself as Frau Mitrofanof. We began to walk towards her apartment without any questions asked. She invited me to join her and stay as long as I needed to; it was with embarrassment and quite apologetically she informed me that unfortunately, food could not be provided, since being alone, she was receiving only one single ration card. This meant that I would have to look for food on my own. "Every restaurant," she quickly added, "provides soup, coffee and beer, free of charge."

I was touched to the core and expressed my gratitude while holding back tears.

One time, as I was in the lineup waiting for soup, somebody offered me a very small loaf of bread, which I greedily held close to my body and cherished the thought of feasting on it with my soup. Yet, I did not have anything to cut the bread with, so I abandoned the thought. I noticed a few steps behind me, a German soldier in a tattered uniform and very tired looking. I approached him, expecting that he would have a penknife. He obliged with a smile, which caused me to cut the tiny loaf in half and offer it to him. I brought the other half to Frau Mitrofanof.

Since I knew that I could not stay forever with Mrs. Mitrofanof, I began to search for some kind of work in Berlin, this brought about my placement in the labour camp of Wilhelmshafen some days later.

On one particular cold winter evening, I was sitting with Frau Mitrofanof and we were drinking a chicory drink which was called coffee. It was warm in the apartment and rather cosy. Finally, there was an opportunity to ask a question I had previously hesitated to pose. She knew that I was Jewish because her daughter told her. Why was she sheltering me, a stranger and a Jew? Why was she risking her life? I made it clear that I was very grateful yet may never be able to reciprocate. I just wondered what made her do it! In response, Mrs. Mitrofanof placed her hand on mine and looked at me very kindly while saying the following: "As you know, my name is Mitrofanof. My husband belonged to Russian nobility. He found himself in your situation during the 1917 Revolution in

Russia when the Communists took over the rule of power. It was a Jewish gentleman who risked his life and brought him out of Russia into Germany. I am now paying the debt."

We both smiled at one another warmly. I was grateful for the discovery and confirmation that in a world filled with murder, robbery, attempt of dehumanization and annihilation, a world so full of incredible horror and dirt, moral debts do exist. Their payments are duly honoured, whilst the memory of them may call for reimbursements offered to others in dire need!

8 | Beauty in the Dirt

In the course of time, I found myself in Wilhelmshafen, a labour camp for Aryans. It needs to be stated that I pretended to be a non-Jew, a *mask* that enabled me to share experiences and also harsh conditions with many young people from several European countries. We were caught, marshalled by the Germans and their collaborators into the ranks of the Organization Todt. We were effectively considered and treated as slaves and existed in the complete and arbitrary service of a ruthless totalitarian state. Many had not survived the work or the war. My own experience included being sent to two camps – Pütnitz and Wilhelmshafen. The Organization Todt managed to aggressively and forcefully seize thousands of young people from everyday activities and transport them into labour camps. In general, they were always shuffling youths from one camp to another as they deemed necessary.

For lack of a better description of the process, I shall reluctantly use the term 'conscription.' Upon 'conscription' into the Organization, one was given an ID card. No compensation existed. They hardly fed us, yet it was a terrific camp life when compared to labour camps meant for Jews. After a hard day's work, we all still had some energy left to sing, play the accordion or harmonica, perhaps even dance in the common hall, called by our captors Kulturhaus. I was with Polish Christian youths some of the time and with German employers at other times, yet always a slave. I avoided contact with my co-workers out of fear of being recognized as a Jew. In consequence, I played the role of a shy, withdrawn, quiet person, present but not participating in any social activities. On one occasion, I sat on a bench in the Kulturhaus and became engrossed in the state of my 'wardrobe.' There was very little to look at. Actually, everything I owned was worn in layers since there were no lockers and that was fine. All I had was a white blouse which was slowly turning grey, a man's jacket, and a kind of German Luftwaffe coat for girls. The most important item worthy of examination was my riding boots, essentially the only footwear I had at the time. Since my feet were always wet and cold, it was necessary to examine the soles. I sat in my multicoloured socks, multicoloured due to a most unusual assortment of coloured threads used to darn them.

I was taking them off when the people around me showed a sudden excitement. A new group of individuals was coming in. They were shouting and laughing, speaking different languages, getting acquainted with the rest of us. Somebody was announcing that they were medical students drafted by the Organization just taken from the streets of various countries in Europe.

As I was sitting there with my condemned boots in hand, I became aware of a young man standing in front of me, looking also at my boots and reaching out for them. Surprised is not exactly descriptive of what I felt; there was anxiety. Was he going to take my boots? He had a pair of military-looking boots over his left shoulder and a pair of boots on his feet. "What did he want with my riding boots?" was the fleeting thought when he actually had one in his hands. I just looked, he smiled at me and pointed to his own boots hanging over his shoulders, a pen knife in his hand motioning what he intended to do. He was trying to tell me that he wanted to pull off the soles of my boots and replace them with those from his spare ones. I finally understood. He took my boots and simultaneously introduced himself in Italian, "I am Mario." Then he gestured asking for my name, to which I replied, "Zofia." This was of course my assumed name and was on the Organization Todt ID document.

Mario left with my boots. There was no conversation possible. We had no verbal language in common. There was a lot of commotion in the place – singing, dancing, laughing – which I observed, even enjoyed. Time elapsed. As I was sitting without actively participating, I had no idea how long it took for Mario to return but there he appeared with my boots properly repaired. Not a word was uttered, only a look and a smile expressed my gratitude. Mario joined the crowd singing and dancing while I quietly left the hall, entered the communal dormitory and occupied a spot on the highest level of the bunks which stood four tiers high. I placed my cherished boots and jacket under my head as a pillow and used the coat as a cover. The cold, damp, poorly lit dorm was the least of my worries at that particular time.

Routinely, the day would start for us at 4:00 AM followed by roll call in the barrack square and then work on wintry roads until darkness fell. The only nourishment was some 'ersatz' coffee, stale bread and a bowl or two of thin watery cabbage soup. Life in Wilhelmshafen was harsh but still bearable and certainly not to be compared with the dreaded 'concentration' or 'death' camps where people, mostly Jews, were systematically killed. I would like to draw attention to the usually employed expression 'exterminated' and wish to distinguish between the two terms 'to kill' and 'to exterminate.' In my understanding, in war, people are killed. In contrast, one exterminates rats, vermin, pests, cockroaches and other parasites. The Nazi consideration of us as sub-human fit their 'extermination' concept. I do hope that people shall be mindful of the difference and respect it. I still hurt when the term 'extermination' is being used. I shudder to think that the death of my people, including my beloved parents and family, is referred to as extermination.

Neither hard work nor poor nourishment has ever bothered me. What evokes abhorrence to this day is the behaviour of the foremen, the corrupt, brutish and uncouth individuals who collaborated with the German authorities.

One evening when I settled in my bunk, I heard the entrance door squeak open slowly; this was followed by quiet long steps, nearing toward the bunk section I was in. My heart began to race. I was afraid the intruder might be one of those foremen who were known to force themselves upon the young girls under their command. Rumour had it that there was not much one could do about it. I held my breath, shut my eyes and just lay there hoping that in the totally dark place, I would not be noticed or targeted. The steps were coming closer, ascending the ladder to where my head lay. I could hear the breathing and felt a gentle touch of a hand on my cheek. I lay there without a sign of life and heard a voice, "Bella, bella, Zofia!" That was all!

It was obvious that it was Mario. He disappeared slowly in the darkness and left me with an indelible impression, the profound memory of great beauty in the midst of dirt.

9 | After Warsaw

THIS STORY BEGINS AFTER THE Warsaw Uprising, which resulted in the evacuation of the entire population from Warsaw to Pruszkow, a special transit camp near Warsaw. I found myself in the midst of crowds of evacuees, including my last employers, where I worked as their child's nanny.

My employers were very quickly released and made their way to Germany. The rest of the people, myself included, had to remain in the camp in order to be classified by the German officers seated at many tables. Their goal was to assess our suitability for various work assignments in Germany.

I found an acquaintance, a neighbour of my employers in the crowd, a lady pharmacist who, like me, was waiting to be 'classified.' It was not a comfortable wait. Neither she nor I wanted to be shipped off to Germany proper. As we waited, we also observed the procedure and noticed that some of the people were being released and were happily leaving the camp grounds. We began to inquire about the reason for those people's release. To our surprise, we discovered that people with serious diseases, the physically and mentally challenged as well as pregnant women were automatically let go.

We, the pharmacist and I, hatched a little plan, since we had nothing to lose and hopefully freedom to gain. We looked at one another critically for a moment: I saw her as a very slim almost emaciated woman who would pass for one suffering from tuberculosis; her tiredness was an added benefit to confirm the claimed diagnosis. I, on the other hand, was a little plump. According to her appraisal, I could be successfully classified as being pregnant. We snickered and decided that it was worth a try. We also decided to avoid appearing at the same table for fear of me bursting out laughing. Each of us went to a different table before a small committee with a physician who asked all the pertinent questions. At one point, I glanced towards the other table and saw my 'partner in conspiracy' moving away with a smile on her face. It took a few more minutes, I was asked some health questions and was let go. The plan worked!

We returned on foot to Warsaw and found it an abandoned city. There were no people on the streets but a lot of dead bodies. We went back to the apartment that had been left empty and open. I gathered a few items that were there: my brown skirt, an ivory silk blouse, a man's grey woollen jacket left there by my employers, some underwear and my riding boots.

Our next steps were toward the estate of my employer's family living some fifty kilometres away from Warsaw. We 'travelled' on foot and, by the grace of some farmers, in their horse-drawn wooden carts. We arrived on the estate of the Lubomirski family, whom we found hospitable and elegant. The experience became incredible! The family lived in style – as though there was no war going on. Their three sons supervised the peasants working on their estate just as they had always done. What we found incredible was the custom of changing into formal attire, for the entire family, for dinner every night! Only some fifty kilometres away was a demolished Warsaw. It would have been a miracle had I continued to live there; fate destined for me a different path.

One day, a party of some twenty German soldiers arrived and proceeded to requisition a part of the estate. They had been ordered to set up a medical-dental clinic to serve members of the German armed forces. They permitted the owners and their family to remain on their estate; everybody else would be evacuated. The lady pharmacist announced that she was leaving to join her family. I was the only stranger-guest there.

The time arrived to examine or interrogate me. My anxiety level rose rapidly. I decided to pretend not to understand a word of German, although I spoke it fluently since I had begun to speak. The use of an interpreter afforded me time to think carefully about the answers I was to give. One slip could have cost my life. A dental surgeon was to be in charge of the clinic. He was present at the interview and spoke immediately following it. He disclosed his need for an assistant who would be more "sensitive both in spirit as much as in touch than the clumsy German soldiers." He looked at me not knowing that I understood what he said and asked whether I would be willing to fill the position, at least for the time being. He made a point of letting me know that he was quite willing to train me. I waited for the translation and graciously agreed to stay.

A few weeks later, I was evacuated, directed to join hundreds of Poles and found myself on a train headed for Poznań, a city in western Poland, close to the German border. A large group of us was taken to the airport and directed to board two planes. I managed to find myself on a half-empty plane; in order to avoid contact with the rest of the crowd, I found a spot at the very back, lay down under an empty seat and remained there during the entire flight. Under the seat I found some items of clothing such as a very well used Luftwaffe coat and a little cap. I inquired if it belonged to anybody, was told that it was abandoned a long time ago and was permitted to take it. On arrival in Frankfurt an der Oder, I was wearing the Luftwaffe coat, the little hat and my riding boots, looking much like a German girl and did not find it difficult to leave the airport by myself, independent of the crowd I wanted to avoid.

10 | Sold on the Open Market

By now, I became one of the Organization Todt slaves. I had been in Wilhelmshafen, a camp for young people gathered in various European countries such as Poland, France, Italy, Norway and Denmark for the purpose of enhancing the war effort. I had been sent to Pütnitz, an army outpost where the majority of workers were German. It seemed that I was the only non-German, non-paid foreigner there and Polish to be exact. By this time, I had gained 'expertise.' That is, if one dares to call my limited experience of a few weeks as a dental assistant in Poland on the Lubomirski estate before I became an evacuee to Germany 'expertise.'

Up to that point, I did not have the actual feel of the centuries-old concept referring to buying or selling people in the slave trade. The railway station of Bremen in Germany taught me quickly about the practice and its reality. I stood with several young people in a row-like order for easy inspection and assessment by prospective buyers. The 'salesmen' circled around us to make sure that their 'merchandise' was well behaved and, most importantly, all present. Every buyer had specifications and every slave a price, an entity never disclosed to the 'merchandise.' I never thought of it before, yet when I write about it, the question arises, "Was

I worth much?" After all I was young, healthy, quite attractive with qualities discoverable only in due course by an interview.

A buyer arrived. He looked intensely at the girls in the group and stopped in front of me, "Sprichst du Deutch?" (Do you speak German?) He asked in a business-like tone and manner. My reaction was resentment and anger. For a short moment, I was indignant and objected to the familiarity of the 'du' expressing his superiority and the right to lack of respect. As strange as it may sound, I was not yet ready to lower my status to one of a subservient slave subject. There was no room in my conscious interaction with a total stranger for acting in compliance with his perception of who I was or ought to have been.

It happened to me before, during the Death March. A German soldier threw at me a very heavy and very dirty rag, which he stumbled upon on the road. I threw it back at him at the risk of being shot. I wondered what made him march as a guard, a 'powerful member of the master race,' without making me die.

On the railway platform of Bremen, I was bought by a man. We walked slowly towards his home in a very stylish apartment building. I realized that he was a high-ranking German officer who lost his arm during the war. He showed me my room as well as the rest of his apartment. I stayed in my room and since I had nothing to unpack, I sat on the bed acquainting myself with the surroundings. It took a little time to realize that there was no key in the door of the bedroom. Almost simultaneously, my 'owner' opened the door in his dressing gown with a smile on his face – just to tell me that I shall like it there and that he considered me to be a very pleasant person. My thoughts at that point were very much mixed. I was fearful of his intentions and helpless in my reaction to an unlawful intruder into my very private and dangerously positioned life. I could avoid intrusion by admitting my being Jewish and remain safe, for a few moments, since to a German at that time, any sexual contact with a Jew was judged to be 'Rassenschande' (defilement of race) which would bring about immediate death. Should I decide to submit, I would die for shame and disgust.

Incredibly, at that very moment, the air-raid sirens began to sound loudly and intensely. I quickly stood up, helped my 'owner' to dress and we speedily joined the gathering crowd in the shelter below street level. The sirens persisted, which gave me time to make a decision to escape the shelter, run to the railway station and disappear. It was perhaps a risky operation to undertake and I did not contemplate alternatives. I was not shrewd enough to have any choices. No matter what I did, it would have been and would continue to be risky.

I told my 'master' that I needed to use the toilet urgently and pressed my way through the crowded bunker. I remembered the way back to the train station from the walk with my 'owner' and ran as quickly as I could without even looking back. I ran through the empty streets, reached the station quickly without any difficulty. The sirens were still piercingly loud and long.

I swiped the Organization Todt ID at the wicket in a way that hid the print on its cover and shouted that I had to get that particular train which was waiting on the platform. Nobody stopped me. The train began to move and I discovered that it was filled with German military, without any civilian passengers.

I was horrified. What business does a civilian have on a military train? I was afraid to take a seat in case one would start a conversation. I decided to move continuously, as if doing some specific task, necessitating reaching the end compartment and returning to the first one, as if on some assigned mission. The train was full. Both seats and gangways were tightly occupied with soldiers standing in close proximity to each other. I was hiding in full view, being on the move and saying, "Entschuldigen sie bitte," which means, "Excuse me, please! Excuse me, please!" I repeated this every few meters in order to get through. The train finally stopped some distance beyond a railway station in Westfalia. The name of the place was Altenhudem. It was the first stop since Bremen. I stepped down from the train, noticed a huge boulder, sat down on the grass beneath it and waited for the train to leave.

I remained there, seated inconspicuously, and dug a hole big enough with my hand to bury my Organization Todt identity card in it.

Many years later, I returned to the same spot, in 1985, with my husband. The ID was of course not there. I wondered impishly who could have taken it. We looked at one another, the view around us, and burst out laughing with a happy, joyful laugh.

11 | I Knew Who I Was

I HAPPENED TO BE IN Kirchhundem, Germany, a village near Altenhundem, still under an assumed identity, working in a household, attending church with the family and making some potentially dangerous mistakes in the observance of Catholic rituals. One of those observances that could have cost my life was my ignorance of the 'communion' procedure. We were approaching the priest in the usual lineup in order to receive the piece of 'wafer' on the tongue. I was not given it! Nobody remarked on it until we left the church. On the way home, the lady of the house, where I was working, curiously raised a question, "Why did you not remove your gloves when approaching the priest for communion?" "Oh ... this is why I did not receive the communion!" I retorted. "Well, this is how it is done in Poland where I come from, we always try to be as elegant as possible and my gloves are the only piece which I consider more elegant than the rest of me. My hands are not exactly nice enough." We all laughed and I assured them that it would not happen again.

In the course of time, the American troops came in and I didn't have to worry about going to church. I continued to work and avoided any remarks in regard to the possible signs of the war ending, until some weeks later the British troops replaced the American troops and established the BAOR (British Army of the Rhine) Training Centre in Bad Lippspringe.

It was difficult for me to adjust to the idea of not having to be afraid. There was no room for me to express any thoughts about the changes taking place, nor was there room for showing my delight due to those changes. My German employers were anxious, reluctant to even acknowledge the possibility of German defeat and I respected that.

One day, announcements were being made by the British who were inviting all DPs (displaced persons) in the area, to be greeted by them and to receive a bottle of wine per person provided by the local winery. All DPs ran and so did I. The crowd and commotion were horrendous. Everybody was leaving happily carrying a bottle of wine. Everybody, that is, but me. There I stood at the entrance of a huge hall shocked and amazed that there were no more bottles. Not even one single bottle for me! As I stood there, I said to myself, but obviously loud enough to be heard, "And I became nothing?!" Of course, I meant that I didn't get anything. My English was obviously inadequate, which made me use the German word 'bekommen,' meaning 'to get.' Out of nowhere, from the farthest door of the huge hall, came a loud and clear question: "And what did you want to become?" The voice was followed by a smiling officer who approached me while I, embarrassed by my mistake and not being able to correct it, requested the services of an interpreter. Indeed an interpreter was available. The three of us sat down. Both British gentlemen began to inquire about me. When I informed them about being Jewish, the officer said, almost in a whisper, "Keep it under your hat. We don't yet know where we are at," and followed with more questions which resulted in a most wonderful, as much as unexpected: "How long do you think it will take you to improve your English?" I was stumped. How would I know? I only had some school English but I could speak German, Russian and Polish fluently. Before I managed to answer and express my doubt whether I was able to improve my English altogether or if ever, the officer spoke up in a matter-of-fact way: "I'll give you a month. Where do you live?" They said they would pick me up in a month's time at 4:00 PM on a certain date. "We will be in a black Mercedes Benz and we will drive past your address and stop a little farther past your house in order not to draw much attention to ourselves or to you entering a car with British soldiers in it."

It was difficult to believe that they would even remember me in a month's time. I began to work feverishly on improving my English with a young German lady whose one important characteristic was a patch on one eye, which she lost during the war. We had lessons whenever we were both free. Another trait that became quite evident was her extraordinary patience and kindness in her devotion to help me learn. Her name was Gertrud Behle.

My second educational resource was a group of soldiers guarding the wine cellar. I used to engage them in very simple conversations and they offered to correct my vocabulary and grammar as well as my pronunciation. It was fun to actually 'converse' with them. They used an unsophisticated English employing expressions like 'bloody' or 'damn' which I did not distinguish from other unfitting words but it did not seem to matter at that point in my 'career' … or did it?

On one occasion, I was interpreting at an international conference of representatives debating the contribution and food distribution for DPs, and the needs of Germany's population. In that particular instance, I was interpreting from Russian to English. I was sitting between the Russian officer on my right and an English officer on my left. I turned, faced the English officer and very innocently said, "The bloody Russian captain says...." " To my astonishment the English captain gasped in horror, "Sophie!" At that moment, I understood the blunder I made. Everyone, including myself, burst into spontaneous laughter when they saw my red face. Thanks to the sense of humour in the British Army, that particular incident did not jeopardize my 'career.'

As promised, the Mercedes Benz arrived at 4:00 PM on the appointed day. It was not difficult to enter the car without drawing attention in the neighbourhood. We began to chat in the car, mostly unimportant small talk, yet important enough to assess my fluency in English. We were joined by another officer on arrival at the military centre. The outcome was very positive; I was invited to accompany them to different meetings that involved travelling in tanks with frequent translations into German, Polish and Russian. I was advised to move away from my employers and live with a German family in their beautiful home. It seemed incredible, almost surreal, when the British military informed me that the German home owners would vacate the main floor, move to the top floor and look after me! They would clean, cook, do laundry and see to it that I enjoyed comfort and peace.

To my delight, I noticed a piano, which promised me a return to normality. My first thought was to hire a piano teacher and continue the process of emotional rehabilitation. I had to cling to something positive and creative. Shedding the fear of impending punishment for being Jewish, I needed to revive some aspect of creative endeavours that had to be hidden as much as denied – all in the effort to mask who I was. Yet throughout that whole long period, I never forgot who I was! The rest was careful, precise acting. It seemed difficult to ignore situations in which I risked being caught 'red handed' in activities which would unmask my act as a maid, a cleaning lady, a nanny, or what have you.

On one such occasion, on a morning in Warsaw, when my employers were out, I was tidying and cleaning the living room which housed a beautiful grand piano. The fact that I was a conservatory graduate could not be revealed, even to myself – but on that particular day, I could not resist the temptation and played until I heard the sound of the key in the entrance door; I closed the piano as quickly as possible and restarted the vacuum. At that very moment, the couple entered and the gentleman remarked: "There was some beautiful piano playing as we were coming up the stairs, did you hear?" There were several suites in the apartment block described in Polish as 'kamienica,' which means a 'building of stone.' Given the fact that there were other flats within very close proximity, without directly stating it, I implied it was a possible explanation and in a very coy manner replied, "Oh, I thought I heard something, but I had to continue vacuuming." Being careful not to disclose interest in the matter, I added, "Where was the music coming from?" To this day, I believe that he may have suspected me but he never let on.

Another danger stemmed from a simple duty, which was assigned by my employer, to select books for her at the library. I thoroughly enjoyed this task and chose books that I would have liked to read. One day, when she showed her anger and frustration with my choices, I had an answer; "It was the librarian who gave them to me, when I said that the books were for *my lady*." She wanted to believe me; it was flattering to her, nonetheless she began to visit the library herself.

These occurrences remain a memory one wants to smile about today. Freedom was at hand yet I was still warned to keep my identity a secret.

It was an interesting time. Daily, we were travelling in tanks, examining the countryside, visiting administrative buildings and offices, especially those essential for establishing contact with the German local authorities, the Bürgermeister, where my ability to speak the language was helpful and less threatening since I was a civilian who did not represent an occupying authority. We also made a point of making contact with DP camps in the neighbouring villages, engaged the displaced people in conversation, offered help in communication wherever and whenever possible and most of all, in my case, having an opportunity of finding survivors, hoping to find a family member, a friend, another Jew.

One day, I was introduced to a British captain who was a Jewish physician. He just happened to be the first Jew I met after the war. The feeling was exhilarating to the point that I spontaneously kissed his hand and heard him say, "Are you sure you have no venereal disease?" I looked at him and said absolutely nothing!

Yes, he was tactless, yet he was well informed about some more of the inhuman treatment Jews had to endure. The German authorities had indeed made arrangements for supplying their soldiers with opportunities for sexual outlets by using very young, beautiful and innocent Jewish girls as prostitutes by force. The payment? ... more degradation, more fear of death when judged by the 'users' as inadequate in performance, and eventual venereal illness, death by flogging or, whenever possible, suicide.

When I think about it today, as I write, I wonder how Nazi ideology dealt with their philosophical concept of 'Rassenschande.' Hitler's sick mind was not able to perceive the tragic truth that by wanting to establish the Germans as the 'Herrenrasse,' an elite or superior race, he made them live with the lowest level of integrity, if at all, in every area of behaviour, certainly lower than human.

Unlike Hitler, for whom a titmouse is only a titmouse, I am unable to make comparisons among lower forms of animal species due to lack of expertise in that area.

12 | BAD LIPPSPRINGE

THE BAOR (BRITISH ARMY OF THE RHINE) Training Centre was ready for operation. I was asked to continue with my work as a law-court interpreter and assume additional duties, namely dealing with the German personnel employed at the centre. I was all of twenty-two years old, with no qualifications, which may have been required for successful fulfilment of my duties. All I had was a hope that somehow I would learn by 'doing.'

It was incredible for me to be starting a normal life, having my own office, my own work, responsibilities and people relying on my input. It felt good! I enjoyed being alive! I began to mix with the local population and made friends with some. To my astonishment, I did not feel anger, neither did I wish to avoid or ignore the people who were trained and indoctrinated with the ideology of their superiority as a race. On occasion, I was informed of difficulties some of the German families had. I understood that it was my duty and privilege to help them.

What I wonder about now was my ability to ignore the loss of everything and everybody dear to me: my parents, family, friends and people I loved, my home. I was never able to openly mourn the loss of my own past activities, pleasures, expressions of thoughts or even my particular sense of humour. All was or seemed to be a blank. I never cried. I never reminisced. I was never homesick or ever depressed. I must have decided to invest my energy in building a future. Essentially there was nobody I could rely on. For years, my Jewishness was to be kept hidden – but my traits, thinking, philosophy of life were very much coming to the fore. The values instilled and all that was taught to me at home became a guideline (a plumb line, a moral compass) to much of my behaviour. They were the foundation of all the planning and execution of what needed to be done or needed to be avoided. I remember a small verse written by my mother into a diary or what may have been a collection of thoughts. In translation from Polish it sounds as follows:

> *If you want to be happy and a miracle behold;*
> *Remain a faithful daughter in the Jewish fold.*

— 1948

Another thought expressed an affable approach to dealing with life's circumstances:

It is more beneficial to be constantly reminded of what one has instead of longing for what one has lost.

With regard to the usually advocated principle of sharing, I was taught to give in a way that would make the recipient feel he or she was doing me a favour by accepting my gift.

One such episode took place whilst we were in the Lwów Ghetto. Both financially and materially we were entirely depleted. A school friend of mine came to our room with very little clothing on her back. She was hungry and very sorrowful. She recounted to us that her parents had been taken away just a few days earlier. I will never forget that scene. It was a tragedy repeated by all of us all too frequently. As she was talking, I prepared the little meal and my mother was laying out my wardrobe – if one could call it that. She was dividing it into two piles. One was offered to my friend. My mother saw to it that certain items fit her and she expressed delight that they did.

That evening, when we were alone, I reproached my mother for giving my friend all the best items while I was left with the old stuff. My mother's response still rings in my memory. She said, albeit with tears in her eyes, "This poor girl has nothing. She has no one left in her life. Would you want her to feel like a beggar in addition to being hungry, cold and all alone? You still have me! I hope that you will always remember what just transpired and learn to appreciate that she did you a favour by receiving your clothes."

On another occasion, I objected to our sharing whatever we had since nobody ever reciprocated. I learned a beautiful lesson when I heard my mother say, "We do not give to have somebody reciprocate. Let us hope that they will share with someone else who will need it equally or more than we do."

My family believed in the value of learning. No amount of wealth impressed either of my parents. I was reminded throughout my youth, that nobody could deprive you of what you have learned and who you are. Only learning is the key to independence and spiritual power ready to share and use for a world in constant need of repair. I remember it well.

The time came to plan my future. I thought of many ways that would enable me to study and work but most of all it was important for me to be who I was born to be without having to pretend and fear disclosure. I could have entered any university and any faculty in Germany but on examination of the possibilities, I chose a way that enabled my very honest desire to shed any trace of pretence – role-playing or manoeuvring to fit into society which were alien and/or possibly hostile to me and my people. The thought occurred that education is more than instruction leading to one's profession. I asked how a people, who were murdering my people, without opposition from their compatriots, especially those in possession of university degrees, could possibly educate anyone! This kind of thinking removed me from the option of remaining in Germany, obtaining any financial assistance and/or studying there.

It was by pure serendipity that my plans were formulated and brought to a successful meaningful life direction. One particular day, I was having lunch in the 'Officers Mess' of the BAOR Training Centre and happened to glance at a popular women's magazine, which interested me because of its fashion pictures and advertisements, not to mention the depiction of contemporary life in England. There was one advertisement that caught my eye: '*Train To Be A Nurse. Write without obligation to the Ministry of Health, London SW1 England.*'

I promptly wrote and awaited a response with eager anticipation. Several weeks transpired without any reply but I did not give up hope that one might be forthcoming. I was preparing mentally to become a nurse. It would help me, I assumed, to avoid uncomfortable situations during a period of acculturation to an unfamiliar world. As a nurse, I would be studying, having a place to live, and an opportunity to serve those who needed honest compassionate help which would be administered unconditionally. Above all, I was hoping that this kind of genuine service would free me to be myself and lessen the anxiety of pretence in role-playing.

At that very time, I discovered that a little hospital was being built for the exclusive use of British families joining their sons and husbands who were serving in Germany within the parameters of the BAOR Training Centre. I thought that it would be wise to become familiar with customs, terminology, hierarchies and practice at a hospital before commencing formal training in England. I dared to visit the hospital and offer my services if needed. The reception was wonderful. There were only two nurses on duty, a fact which curtailed their freedom to sleep, rest or simply go out if desired. They welcomed my offer with enthusiasm. I took a month's leave from my duties at the BAOR Training Centre and reported for night duty some days later.

On my very first evening on duty, a young English woman who had suffered a broken jaw in a car accident was admitted from another hospital. She was conscious, needed attention and care. Since her jaw was wired, she was unable to talk, eat or even drink without watchful and careful assistance. Her care became my task, under supervision, of course. Several days later she began to talk through clenched teeth since her jaw was still wired. Her first question was direct, dictated by curiosity about my role in her nursing care since I had neither uniform nor badge to display my 'professional' identity. "Who are you," she asked, despite a tightly shut jaw, "and what are you doing here?!" I was happy to hear her voice and pleased to respond in very short sentences that I wanted to become a nurse and stressed that I was expecting, but had not yet received, a reply from the British Ministry of Health to an application for nursing training. In my wildest imagination, I could not have dreamt of having heard her exclaim, "No wonder! Your letter is most certainly on my desk in London!" She asked for my name. We did not talk about it anymore.

A few days later, I returned to my office at the BAOR Training Centre. The British lady was discharged from the hospital. It took about three weeks. When the letter of my acceptance arrived, as a student nurse at the most modern St. Helier Hospital, Carshalton, Surrey, England, I initiated a feverish preparation for a journey toward a profession, a beautiful country, normal surroundings and a path to a future I was hoping to build.

13 | ENGLAND

I T DID NOT TAKE LONG to book the passage, by boat and train to London.

It seems that I managed to plan and prepare for what I considered a normal, cultured life. The important issues, i.e. a roof over my head, assurance of a healthy environment, school, hope to gain a respected and admired profession that was considered to be a vocation, gave me confidence and hope of

— 1947

success, except for one very important fact: I was still Zofia Wolanowska, a Catholic Polish girl in accordance with the document I had and wondered how to deal with this fact. It was difficult to shed a disguise that so far helped me avert discrimination and allowed me to complete my studies, possibly without interruption. Above all, I was hoping to establish a direct and very honest relationship with other human beings through service for them without feeling threatened.

The reality of not being able to continue schooling as a Jew was imprinted in my memory. The anxiety was an expected consequence based on my war experiences. I decided to continue without changing personal data as long as necessary since I did not know the attitudes and laws of English institutions.

It was spring 1947. There seemed to be no major difficulties in being a student nurse. As silly as it may sound, I somehow resented the level of the team that I belonged to and was

— 1947

unable to interact as would be expected of me. This notwithstanding, everybody was polite, kind, tactful yet distant. It
was refreshing to discover that intrusion was not an English
characteristic. Nobody asked personal questions. Studies were
going well. Hospitable, comfortable to live amongst, England
and the English allowed me to feel normal and free for the first
time in many years. I shall always be grateful for the freedom
I felt.

The only problem I had was connected to my hospital's rule
which forbade the student nurses to remain and occupy their
rooms at the time of their vacations. Everybody except myself
was able to go home whilst I for obvious reasons had to find my
own solution. There was no room for discussion and no leeway
for exceptions. I had to find work, a difficult task when our
vacations were short and did not allow for permanence. I was
mostly able to fill the temporary need by being a mother's
helper or a caregiver to the elderly whereby families were able
to have a rest without disturbing the daily order and routine.

LIFE WAS SATISFYING. There were no particular upheavals.
There was no time to reminisce or feel sorry for myself. I
enjoyed living and I loved life, yet I continued to feel uneasy
hiding my identity, as if I were living behind a mask and fearing
its removal. Fate prepared a scene, which could not have been
better choreographed, to remove the mask and let me face the
world with courage, ready to act out an age-old reality.

It happened in 1951. By then I was fully trained as a nurse
and midwife. I sat with several nurses, physicians and students
one day, relaxing over a cup of tea when out of the blue, one of
them declared, "What a pity that Hitler did not kill all Jews."
To my amazement, nobody reacted ... until I looked directly at
the individual who spoke and very slowly asked, "Why do you

think it would have been a good thing to have happened?" The answer came quickly and convincingly; "Because the Jews are a lazy lot. They only want to be doctors, lawyers, accountants – Have you ever seen a Jewish nurse?"

"You are looking at one," I said slowly and matter-of-factly.

Nobody moved. Nobody spoke. I continued by inviting them all to my room. We stopped at the door that displayed my name – Zofia Wolanowska. I took the card down, turned it over and wrote – Gertruda Osterman!

The rest of the story is immaterial. Finally, I stood there smiling, the mask disintegrated. It was gone, no longer there. I wish that we could say with conviction and ease, that the end

— 1947

of the Second World War taught people to treat one another with love, the kind of love that involves care and sensitivity to one's needs, knowledge of the other, and above all, but not in isolation, the respect due to all of us for no other reason but one: we are all, without exception, children of one Almighty God. I see danger in burying humanness and the values inherent in it. It is no secret that what the Jews experienced stems from hatred, indifference and a dismal lack of the knowledge contained in our history. I am too often shocked by people's ignorance of the Shoah, characterized by reversal of the generally known moral code and its consequence expressed in the word Shoah, the Hebrew word for destruction. I would like to believe that the Jewish experience has been, throughout history, characterized by some nobility and a lot of tragedy. Since the first fall of Jerusalem and in various cultures throughout the world, we have endured much persecution and ostracism … with a great deal of indifference expressed by the observing masses.

Can one consider the fact that for many, myself included, our identity as members of a nation, with our particular monotheism, has continued to exist, to be a fluke, an accidental advantage, a lucky stroke?

Writing these stories in which I, a Jew, played a role, I always repeated to myself one important thought: there were many of us, each one fighting for life, who hoped that there eventually would be a better world. May one hope that those of us who became educators, religious leaders, health professionals, politicians have the power to stop or better still prevent irrational hatred? Possibly, if we put our trust in the power of truth to drive out falsehood and the twisting, manipulating, denying and omitting of historical facts. Unadulterated truth must become available and of course appreciated.

14 | THE HERMIT

IT WAS A BEAUTIFUL MORNING in October 1942. We were located in the Lwów Ghetto. My father was no longer with us. It was my mother and I who were forced out of our home and joined many other Jews into a crowded, uncomfortable room. The German occupation law forced us, by that time, to wear a white arm band with a blue Star of David on it. Our identity cards carried a large J for 'Jude,' which made us stand out no matter where we were.

On that particular morning, I decided to deliver some food to the work units that had been sent out from Janowska Concentration Camp. They were working in different parts of the city under strict supervision of the concentration-camp guards. I left my identity card and my armband, which was an important part of my wardrobe, in the ghetto and dared to break the law, which marked us as Jews, in order to move freely from one part of the city to another in search of these units. I was carrying a picnic basket belonging to my mother. Inside there were some precious bits of food that I had collected from friends and neighbours in the ghetto. Food of any kind was painfully scarce! Jews did not have any ration cards, as other Polish people had.

When I was a little girl, I owned a picnic basket of my own, a small replica of my mother's larger one. I used to carry it proudly whenever I would visit the poor with my mother to distribute gifts of food and clothing in the underprivileged section of our city.

But today, on this beautiful October morning in Poland, I was embarking on my own mission of mercy of a very different kind. We knew that the Janowska Concentration Camp was located not far from the centre of our city and that many Jews were incarcerated there.

We were almost certain that among them was my young cousin Joel. There were rumours that parties of inmates from the camp were taken every day to the hills, on the outskirts of the city, to carry out forced labour. My goal was to find one of these work units and somehow manage to make some of the meagre food available to them. Though I couldn't approach them directly, it was my hope that if I left the food along the roadside, they might find it.

It was a dangerous exploit. I knew that if I were to have been caught supplying food to the inmates, I too may have been seized, imprisoned or killed. I walked for some time into the hills, not having any idea where I would find the workers. Suddenly I noticed a little hut in the distance. As I drew closer, I saw a goat, a little dog and some pails of water on the ground. This was an indication that somebody was living there. Just then, an old man came out of the hut. I approached him with the thought that he may be a hermit. "Good afternoon," I said politely. "Don't say that," he replied. "Say 'God be with you.'"

"God be with you," I repeated. Then I asked, "Have you by any chance seen a work group in this neighbourhood? It is possible that they might be labouring out here in the countryside."

"Yes," he replied. "I have seen them. But you will have to climb a bit higher. I saw them passing by, earlier this morning, and I have not yet seen them come down."

"Thank you. Thank you very much," I said.

To which he replied, "Don't thank me. Say 'God reward you.'"

"May God reward you," I repeated. As I was leaving, he asked me to come and see him again on my way back. I promised that I would – his hut would be a landmark for me!

I continued to climb until the work party came in sight. Then, I emptied my basket and laid little packages of food on the ground beside the trail I thought they would be taking. My hope was that the inmates would see the food first and get at least a few bites of it. Thoughts raced through my mind that if the guards saw the food first it was very likely that the men would get nothing. It wasn't that the guards needed the extra food, but quite likely would have had great pleasure in throwing it away just beyond the reach of the starving men.

On my way down, I stopped again at the hut and said to the old man, "Well, here I am." Kindly, he asked me if I found them. "Yes, I saw them from a long distance away and I left the food along the side of the trail in the grass hoping that some individuals would discreetly bend down, pick up some of the packages and benefit from them."

"You are a very courageous little girl," he said.

I became quite indignant. It was undeniably true that I was little. I stood just five feet, two inches tall but I felt very grown up.

"I am not a little girl. I am twenty years old," I quickly retorted.

"To me you seem like a little girl all the same." Then quite unexpectedly his countenance changed and he looked at me in a rather unyielding way, fixing his eyes directly at mine and said in a sobering manner, "You and your people are going through a very hard time now. But you will survive and you will go west. First, you will cross a small body of water. Then, you will cross a large body of water. Don't ever go east for that would only bring you sorrow. You will endure many painful hardships but in the end you will find peace and love and happiness."

I stood there at the time quite surprised and somewhat perplexed by all he had just said. I had no way of knowing then that the words he so solemnly spoke would come to pass exactly as he predicted.

Afterword

DR. TRUDA ROSENBERG's *Unmasked* gave me an unexpected opportunity to hear firsthand the stories of her life; the daring escapes, exploits, the incredible experiences of a young Jewish girl living through the holocaust.

I first met Truda at a Jewish-Christian dialogue group where I was an invited speaker. On closer acquaintance, she shared many of her stories and her intention to write about them. I offered to assist her in this project.

It has been an unparalleled experience for me to have spent the last year aiding Truda in recording her stories, which she wrote by hand and then dictated to me. To have heard each one firsthand, to have watched her relive her memories through tears, bittersweet joy and yes, even laughter, was a journey in itself.

As I listened to Truda's stories, I began to ask myself questions and still wonder how anyone, having experienced and witnessed such cruel and irrational hatred, can live a normal life. The answer came as I reflected on the Hebrew prophet Isaiah who so beautifully expressed in chapter 61:1-3

> *The spirit of the Sovereign Lord is upon me, because*
> *the Lord has anointed me to … comfort all who*

> mourn, to provide for those who grieve in Zion, to
> bestow on them a crown of beauty instead of ashes,
> the oil of gladness instead of mourning, and
> a garment of praise instead of a spirit of despair.
> They will be called oaks of righteousness, the
> planting of the Lord for the display of His splendor.

Indeed, a crown of beauty for ashes! It accentuates the treasure and gift that she is. It speaks of the faith she embraces. Truda always knew who she was and in keeping with her mother's parting words – never let anything happen to her Jewish soul!

Annie Elliott
Director, For Zion's Sake International

About the Author

— 2007

TRUDA ROSENBERG IS A psychologist, educator and storyteller. Of her war experience, she writes:

> It took a very long time to decide on writing a history, albeit of my own experiences during the Shoah. I do not consider myself a writer, and prefer to state that I am a storyteller.

> The few stories presented in this work are authentic episodes that hopefully describe essential instances I experienced as one of many of my people. It is important to stress that at no time did I or do I label my experiences as unique. Their existence is a fact and is presented here as an eyewitness account, a variant picture, which many of us encountered on a daily basis. Some of us were able to deal with the enemy's inhuman need to destroy us; many succumbed and lost the battle; others emerged as victors; still others are making an effort to live in spite of their tragedies. I was able to

escape incarceration in a concentration camp, with its brutal attack on human dignity and bodily endurance in the face of nourishment deprivations and illness, which would have contributed to an inability or lack of will-power to fight.

During the Shoah, I was living under three consecutive identities. When asked to what I attribute my survival, I answer without hesitation: "I knew who I was." This kept me fighting for life and survival as a human being with the celebration of life that I was taught, with a love of people and a love of life. This, to me, is survival.

Having served as a law-court interpreter for the British forces on the Rhine, Dr. Rosenberg trained in nursing and midwifery after the war. In 1951 she emigrated to Vancouver, B.C., where she became a public-health nurse. In 1958 she moved to Ottawa, worked for the Health Department while continuing her studies and graduated with a PhD in psychology in 1971. In 1971 she taught in Israel in the Department of Education and Psychology at Haifa University, and directed the Psychology Department, which she established at Kibbutz Ein Harod. She was, in addition, the chief clinical psychologist for a large mental-health centre and psychiatric hospital in Tirat Hacarhel.

On returning to Ottawa with her husband, Imrich Yitzhak Rosenberg, who was invited to join the Canadian Refugee Advisory Committee, Dr. Rosenberg opened a private practice in clinical psychology. To this day, she is an active, international lecturer and still maintains her practice in Ottawa. *Unmasked* is her first book. In 2007–08 she was a scholar in residence in the School of the Humanities at Carleton University.

Unmasked
First edition | First printing

This book was designed and typeset by Suzanne Burkill in the
spring of 2009. It was printed, Smyth-sewn, and bound by
Coach House Printing, Toronto. The type is Goudy, 11 / 15.
The text stock is Zephyr Antique Laid. Cover sketch of
Truda Rosenberg by Toby Rosenbloom, 2009.